Chapter 1: Recognizing Your Triggers

Procrastination doesn't happen out of nowhere. It's often triggered by specific emotions, circumstances, or thought patterns that create resistance to taking action. In this chapter, we'll explore what those triggers are, how self-awareness can help you recognize them, and finally, walk you through a practical exercise called the Trigger Tracker. By the end, you'll have a clearer understanding of why you procrastinate and how to overcome it.

First, let's talk about triggers. These are the emotional or mental barriers that cause you to delay action. Some common examples include fear, feeling overwhelmed, or simply a lack of motivation. Fear can take many forms, whether it's fear of failure, fear of judgment, or even fear of success. Overwhelm often arises when tasks feel too big or too numerous, leaving us paralyzed and unsure of where to begin. And then there's lack of motivation—when we just don't see the value in a task, it becomes easy to push it aside.

Now, let's dive into self-awareness. This is the foundation for breaking free from procrastination. Without understanding our habits and thought patterns, we remain in the dark about why we procrastinate. Think about your own patterns. Do you avoid tasks that feel too risky? Do you find yourself procrastinating more at certain times of day or in certain environments? Self-awareness allows you to spot these patterns and take control.

To help you recognize and address your triggers, I've created a step-by-step exercise called the Trigger Tracker. Here's how it works. First, start keeping a journal to record moments of procrastination. Each time you delay a task, write down the date and time, the task you avoided, what you did instead, and most importantly, what emotions or circumstances led to that decision. Was it fear? Overwhelm? Maybe you were distracted by something in your environment.

After one week of tracking, review your entries. Look for recurring patterns. Are certain tasks or emotions always linked to procrastination? Once you've identified these triggers, it's time to find solutions. For example, if fear is a trigger, try reframing failure as an opportunity to learn. If you're often overwhelmed, break big tasks into smaller steps. And if lack of motivation is the issue, connect the task to a larger goal or reward yourself for small wins.

By completing this exercise, you'll gain a clearer understanding of your procrastination triggers and how to address them. Remember, awareness is power. Once you know what's holding you back, you can take the first steps toward overcoming it.

Chapter 2: Setting Clear and Realistic Goals

"When your goals are clear, the journey doesn't feel as overwhelming. Clarity is the antidote to procrastination, and in this chapter, we're going to figure out exactly how to create it."

Why Clarity Matters

Let's start with a question: Have you ever set a goal like "get healthier" or "be more productive," but then… nothing happened? You felt stuck, maybe even paralyzed. Why? Because the goal was so vague that your brain didn't know what to do with it.

Here's what happens: When a goal is unclear, your mind sees it as a threat. It's not laziness; it's your brain protecting you from uncertainty and the potential of failure. So, instead of taking action, you avoid it altogether. You scroll through social media, clean your desk, or watch a show you've already seen five times. Sound familiar?

Now, imagine if that goal wasn't vague. What if, instead of "get healthier," you said, "Go for a 20-minute walk on Monday, Wednesday, and Friday this week." It's specific, it's clear, and—most importantly—it feels doable. That's the power of clarity.

The Connection Between Vague Goals and Procrastination

Think about this: If I asked you to "write a book," where would you even begin? Do you outline first? Research? Or just start typing? That kind of ambiguity can make the task feel like climbing a mountain with no map.

But if I said, "Write the first 500 words of your introduction by Friday," suddenly the task feels achievable. You've got a starting point and a clear destination. Clarity transforms your goals from overwhelming to actionable.

Breaking Down Big Goals

Big goals are like puzzles. If you try to tackle the whole thing at once, it's overwhelming. But when you break it into smaller pieces, suddenly, it's manageable.

Let's take an example: Say you want to launch an online store. That's a big goal, right? It's exciting, but where do you start? Here's how to break it down:

1. First, research your target audience.
2. Then, choose a product niche.
3. Register a domain name.
4. Set up your e-commerce platform.
5. And finally, launch your first marketing campaign.

Each of these steps is small and actionable. You're not building the store all at once—you're taking it one step at a time.

The SMART Goals Framework

Now that you've broken your goal into smaller steps, let's make those steps even more powerful with the SMART framework. SMART stands for:

- **Specific:** What exactly do you want to accomplish? Be precise.
- **Measurable:** How will you track your progress?
- **Achievable:** Is the goal realistic given your resources and time?
- **Relevant:** Does this goal align with your larger ambitions?
- **Time-bound:** When will you get it done?

Let's go back to that online store example. A vague goal would be: "Set up a store soon." But a SMART goal would look like this: "Upload five product descriptions to my online store by Friday at noon."

See the difference? It's not just clear—it's actionable. And because it's measurable and time-bound, you can track your progress and stay motivated.

Practical Exercise: Goal Refinement

Let's try this together. I want you to think of a big goal you've been putting off. Got it? Okay, now follow these steps:

1. **Write down the goal.** Start with something big, like "get fit," "finish my thesis," or "start a business."

2. **Break it into smaller tasks.** For example, if your goal is "get fit," your smaller tasks could be:

    o Join a gym.
    o Create a workout schedule.
    o Prepare healthy meals.

3. **Turn each small task into a SMART goal.** Here's an example:

    o Instead of saying, "Join a gym," make it SMART: "Research three gyms in my area and sign up for one by Monday."
    o Or instead of saying, "Start working out," make it SMART: "Do a 20-minute workout on Tuesday, Thursday, and Saturday this week."

4. **Set deadlines.** Give each step a timeline. This keeps you accountable.

Results

So, what happens when you do this? First, you'll feel less overwhelmed. Suddenly, that big goal isn't a mountain—it's a series of small, manageable steps. Second, you'll start building momentum. Each small win will motivate you to tackle the next one. And finally, you'll feel confident, knowing you have a clear, realistic plan to follow.

Remember this: A clear goal is a powerful goal. It's not just something you dream about—it's something you can take action on.

Now, here's your challenge: Take one big goal you've been procrastinating on. Break it down, make it SMART, and take the first step today. Your progress starts right now, with one small, clear action.

"Clarity is the antidote to procrastination. When you know where you're going and how to get there, you've already won half the battle."

Chapter 3: Building Effective Time-Management Skills

Understanding Time as a Resource

Time is the most valuable resource we have—it's finite, irreplaceable, and precious. Yet, so often, we treat it as though we'll always have more.

To take control of procrastination, you must first shift your mindset about time from scarcity to abundance. A scarcity mindset tells you there's never enough time, leading to stress and rushed decisions. In contrast, an abundance mindset helps you see time as something you can manage with intention, giving you a sense of control and empowerment.

Ask yourself this: What if, instead of saying, "I don't have time," you said, "This isn't my priority right now"? It's a subtle change, but it puts you in the driver's seat, showing that time is about choices.

Solution: Start tracking how you currently spend your time. Use a notebook or a time-tracking app to log activities for a week. This will reveal patterns of wasted time and help you make intentional changes. Remember, awareness is the first step toward mastery.

Prioritization Techniques

Procrastination often creeps in when you're overwhelmed with too much to do. Prioritizing tasks helps you focus on what matters most. Two powerful tools to help with this are the Eisenhower Matrix and ABC prioritization.

1. The Eisenhower Matrix This method divides tasks into four quadrants:

- **Urgent and Important:** Do these immediately.
- **Important but Not Urgent:** Schedule these tasks.
- **Urgent but Not Important:** Delegate them if possible.
- **Neither Urgent nor Important:** Eliminate these.

Visualizing your tasks this way helps you focus on long-term goals instead of just reacting to what feels urgent.

2. ABC Prioritization This method involves assigning tasks a grade:

- **A:** Must-do tasks with significant consequences if left undone.
- **B:** Important tasks that can wait but shouldn't be ignored.
- **C:** Low-priority tasks that are nice to do but not essential.

Once categorized, focus on A-tasks first, then move down the list.

Solution: Choose one of these techniques to apply immediately. List your current to-dos and categorize them using either the Eisenhower Matrix or the ABC system. Revisit this list daily to stay on track.

Time-Blocking and Scheduling

Time-blocking is a simple yet transformative strategy. It involves dividing your day into dedicated time slots for specific activities. This method prevents distractions and ensures every task has its moment.

For instance:

5. **8:00–9:00 AM:** Respond to emails.
6. **9:00–11:00 AM:** Work on a priority project.
7. **11:00–11:30 AM:** Take a break or go for a walk.

Key principles:

1. **Be Realistic:** Schedule tasks based on how long they actually take, not how long you wish they'd take.
2. **Batch Similar Tasks:** Group activities like answering emails or brainstorming ideas to maximize focus.
3. **Protect Your Blocks:** Treat your time blocks as appointments. Only reschedule if absolutely necessary.

Solution: At the end of each day, plan the next day's schedule with time-blocking. Review your priorities and assign blocks of time to complete them.

Practical Exercise: Create Your Ideal Weekly Schedule

Now, let's put these strategies into action. Follow these steps to design your ideal week.

Step 1: Brainstorm Your Priorities Write down everything you need to accomplish this week, from work tasks to personal errands. Use the ABC prioritization method to rank them.

Step 2: Allocate Time for Each Priority Estimate how much time each task requires. Then, plot them into a calendar or planner using time blocks. Don't forget to include non-negotiables like meals, sleep, and relaxation.

Step 3: Review and Adjust Look at your schedule. Is it realistic? Are you leaving room for unexpected tasks or downtime? Adjust as needed to create a balanced plan.

Step 4: Follow Your Plan For one week, commit to sticking to your ideal schedule. At the end of the week, reflect on what worked and what didn't. Use these insights to refine your approach.

Results

By following these steps, you'll notice immediate benefits. Tasks that once felt overwhelming become manageable. Distractions have less power over you because every moment has a purpose. And most importantly, you'll regain the confidence and control to make the most of your time.

Remember, time management isn't about doing more—it's about doing what matters. With these techniques, you're not just managing time; you're taking the first step toward a life of focus and intentionality.

Chapter 4: Overcoming Mental Barriers

Welcome to Chapter 4: Overcoming Mental Barriers.

In this chapter, we'll explore the internal struggles that keep us trapped in cycles of procrastination. These mental barriers—like self-doubt, perfectionism, and fear of failure—can feel overwhelming, but with the right mindset and tools, you can break free and move forward with confidence.

We'll tackle four key strategies to overcome these barriers: **challenging negative thought patterns, reframing tasks, practicing self-compassion,** and a powerful exercise to create **positive affirmations.** Let's dive in.

Challenging Negative Thought Patterns

First, let's talk about negative thought patterns. Many of us procrastinate because of unhelpful beliefs that tell us we're not good enough, not capable, or that failure is inevitable. These thoughts often manifest as **self-doubt, perfectionism,** or **fear of failure.**

Identifying the Barriers

- **Self-Doubt:** You might think, "I'm not smart enough to do this," or, "I don't have the skills."
- **Perfectionism:** You set impossibly high standards, convincing yourself that if something isn't perfect, it's not worth doing.
- **Fear of Failure:** You avoid starting because the thought of failure feels unbearable.

The Solution: Replacing Negative Thoughts with Truths

Here's how you can begin challenging these patterns:

- **Identify the Thought:** Pause and ask yourself, "What am I thinking or feeling right now that's causing me to avoid this task?"
- **Question the Thought:** Is this belief based on facts or assumptions? For instance, is it true that you're not capable, or are you just feeling unprepared?
- **Replace the Thought:** Replace it with a more empowering truth. Instead of "I'll never get this done," tell yourself, "I may not know everything now, but I can learn as I go."

Remember, your thoughts are powerful—but you have the power to change them.

Reframing Tasks

Next, let's talk about how we view the tasks in front of us. A lot of procrastination stems from seeing tasks as burdens, something you **have to** do, rather than something you **choose to** do.

The Power of Choice

Consider the difference between these two statements:

8. "I have to write this report."
9. "I choose to write this report because it will help me grow in my career."

By reframing tasks as choices, you remind yourself that you're in control. This simple shift can make even daunting tasks feel more manageable.

The Solution: Connecting Tasks to Your Values

4. Ask yourself, "Why does this task matter to me?"

5. Link the task to a goal, value, or benefit. For example, completing a work project might align with your value of responsibility or your desire for career advancement.
6. Create a reframed statement, like, "I'm choosing to do this because it aligns with my goals and values."

Reframing tasks turns obligations into opportunities.

Practicing Self-Compassion

Now, let's address one of the most critical components: **self-compassion.**

When you procrastinate, it's easy to be harsh on yourself. Thoughts like, "I'm so lazy," or "Why can't I just get it together?" can spiral into shame and frustration. But this approach doesn't help—it only reinforces the cycle of procrastination.

The Power of Forgiveness

Think about how you would comfort a friend who's struggling. You wouldn't berate them. You'd offer support, encouragement, and understanding. You deserve the same kindness from yourself.

The Solution: Shifting to Self-Compassion

1. **Acknowledge the Struggle:** Say to yourself, "Procrastination is hard, but I'm not alone in this. Many people face this challenge."
2. **Forgive Yourself:** Let go of guilt by saying, "It's okay that I've struggled with this. I'm human, and I'm learning."
3. **Encourage Yourself:** Remind yourself of your strengths and progress, no matter how small.

Self-compassion creates the emotional safety you need to grow and improve.

Practical Exercise: Affirmation Creation

Finally, let's create a tool to help you rewire your mindset: **positive affirmations.** Affirmations are simple, empowering statements that counteract negative beliefs.

Steps to Create Your Affirmations

1. **Identify Your Barriers:** Write down the most common negative thoughts you experience when procrastinating.

2. **Reframe the Thought:** For each negative thought, create a positive counter-statement.

    o For example:

    - Negative Thought: "I always fail at big tasks."
    - Affirmation: "I can break big tasks into smaller steps and succeed."
3. **Speak Them Aloud Daily:** Repeat your affirmations each morning or before tackling a challenging task.

Examples of Positive Affirmations

- "I am capable of taking one small step forward, even when I feel stuck."
- "I have the courage to try, even if it's not perfect."
- "Every effort I make moves me closer to my goals."

Affirmations are your mental reset button. Use them to redirect your energy and focus.

Results of Overcoming Mental Barriers

When you challenge your negative thoughts, reframe your tasks, and practice self-compassion, you'll feel a shift. Tasks that once seemed overwhelming become more approachable. You'll develop confidence in your ability to take action, and most importantly, you'll cultivate a kinder, more supportive relationship with yourself.

Remember, procrastination isn't a reflection of your worth—it's a habit you can overcome. The tools in this chapter are the first steps to building that change.

Chapter 5: Creating an Environment for Success

The Impact of Your Surroundings

Narration: "Take a moment to look around you. Is your workspace cluttered with papers, half-empty coffee mugs, and random items that don't belong there? Or is it clean, inviting, and designed to help you focus?

Your environment plays a crucial role in shaping your behavior. Cluttered spaces often lead to a cluttered mind, making it harder to focus and increasing the temptation to procrastinate. Imagine trying to write an important email while your phone buzzes with notifications, and there's a pile of unfinished paperwork screaming for your attention. No wonder it's easier to just scroll through social media instead.

But here's the good news: by intentionally designing your environment, you can set yourself up for success. When distractions are minimized, and your workspace feels inspiring, it becomes easier to stay focused and motivated."

Designing a Productive Workspace

Narration: "Creating a productive workspace doesn't mean buying expensive furniture or fancy gadgets. It's about creating a space that works for you—one that reduces distractions and keeps you in the right frame of mind. Let's break this down into actionable steps:

1. **Declutter Ruthlessly**: Start by removing everything that doesn't belong in your workspace. Toss out old papers, unnecessary knick-knacks, and anything you haven't used in months. If you don't need it to complete your work, it doesn't need to be there.

2. **Organize with Purpose**: Arrange your tools and supplies so they're easy to find. Use trays, drawers, or organizers for items like pens, chargers, and notebooks. Having a designated spot for everything saves you time and mental energy.
3. **Add Elements of Comfort**: A comfortable chair, good lighting, and a proper desk setup can make a world of difference. If you can, position your desk near natural light—it's been shown to improve focus and mood.
4. **Incorporate Inspiration**: Add a few elements that motivate you, like a vision board, an inspiring quote, or even a small plant. These touches can help make your workspace a place you actually enjoy spending time in."

The Role of Digital Tools

Narration: "In today's world, distractions often come in the form of digital interruptions—endless notifications, social media updates, and a constant influx of emails. Managing these distractions is key to staying focused. Here are some tools to help:

- **Focus Apps**: Tools like Forest or Focus@Will can help you stay on task by gamifying focus sessions or providing distraction-free music.
- **Website Blockers**: Use extensions like StayFocusd or apps like Freedom to block distracting websites during work hours.
- **Task Management Systems**: Apps like Todoist, Notion, or Trello can help you organize your tasks and prioritize effectively.
- **Notification Management**: Turn off non-essential notifications on your phone and computer. Set specific times to check emails and messages instead of allowing constant interruptions.

These tools work best when combined with self-discipline. Remember, the goal isn't just to block distractions—it's to build habits that keep you focused."

Practical Exercise: Workspace Makeover

Narration: "Now it's time for a hands-on activity. Grab a pen and paper—or your phone, if that's more convenient—and get ready to transform your space.

10. **Step 1: Evaluate Your Current Workspace**
    Sit in your usual workspace and take note of what feels distracting or disorganized. Ask yourself: What's working? What's not?
11. **Step 2: Clear the Clutter**
    Dedicate 15-30 minutes to declutter. Remove items you don't use, toss out trash, and relocate anything that doesn't belong in your workspace.
12. **Step 3: Reorganize for Functionality**
    Arrange your most-used items within arm's reach. Group similar items together—pens and sticky notes in one container, electronics in another.
13. **Step 4: Add One Inspirational Element**
    Choose one item to make your space more inspiring. It could be a framed photo, a motivational quote, or even a small piece of art.
14. **Step 5: Set Up Digital Boundaries**
    Download a focus app or adjust your notification settings right now. Commit to testing this setup for the next week.
15. **Step 6: Reflect and Adjust**
    After using your revamped workspace for a week, reflect on the changes. Ask yourself: What feels better? Is there anything else you can improve?"

Results: How a Transformed Space Transforms You

Narration: "By the end of this process, your workspace will feel less like a source of stress and more like a tool for success. You'll notice that it's easier to focus, and tasks that once felt overwhelming will feel more manageable. Small changes, like decluttering and using digital tools wisely, can lead to big shifts in your productivity and mindset.

Remember, your environment is a reflection of your goals. When you design it to support your success, procrastination doesn't stand a chance. Let's move forward to the next chapter and continue building the habits that will help you thrive."

Chapter 6: Building Momentum with Small Wins

The Power of Starting Small

Let's start with a question. Have you ever faced a task so overwhelming that you couldn't even bear to start it? Maybe it was an assignment, a project at work, or even something as mundane as organizing your closet. When a task feels too big, it paralyzes us, and procrastination takes over. But here's the secret: you don't have to conquer the mountain in one giant leap. You only need to take the first small step.

Starting small is powerful because it lowers the barrier to entry. By focusing on just one tiny action, you bypass the fear and resistance that come with a massive, undefined project. Small actions also give you quick wins—those little moments of success that provide a rush of accomplishment. These wins release dopamine in your brain, motivating you to keep going.

Think of it this way: a single drop of water might seem insignificant, but over time, drops can carve a path through solid rock. Small actions, consistently repeated, can make an incredible difference.

Micro-Tasks and Quick Wins

The key to starting small is breaking your larger tasks into micro-tasks—bite-sized actions that you can complete in just 5 to 10 minutes.

For example, if your goal is to write a report, don't think about the entire report. Instead, focus on creating the title or writing a single sentence. If your goal is to clean your house, don't aim to clean the whole thing—just focus on clearing one surface, like your desk or kitchen counter.

Quick wins like these are motivational gold. They trick your brain into thinking, "Hey, this wasn't so bad. I can do more." And once you complete one micro-task, it's easier to move on to the next.

Here's an example: imagine you're dreading going to the gym. Instead of committing to a full workout, tell yourself you'll just put on your gym clothes and drive to the gym parking lot. Once you're there, you're more likely to step inside, and before you know it, you're halfway through your workout.

Small tasks eliminate the psychological resistance to starting and build the momentum you need to keep moving forward.

The Snowball Effect

Have you ever seen a snowball rolling downhill? It starts small, but as it picks up speed, it grows larger and larger. This is exactly how momentum works when you focus on small wins.

Each small victory builds your confidence and makes the next step feel easier. Over time, those steps add up to significant progress. It's a cumulative effect—one that transforms daunting goals into achievable milestones.

The snowball effect also works as a motivator because it reinforces a positive identity. For instance, if you consistently complete small tasks toward studying, you begin to see yourself as someone who is disciplined and dedicated. This identity shift keeps you committed to your goals and helps you avoid falling back into procrastination.

Practical Exercise: Take One Small Step

Now, it's your turn to take action.

Think about a task or goal that you've been putting off. It could be something as simple as replying to an email, starting a new hobby, or organizing your files. Got it? Great. Now ask yourself:

What is the smallest possible step I could take toward completing this task?

For example:

- If you've been avoiding cleaning your house, your first step could be picking up one piece of clutter.
- If you need to write a paper, your first step might be opening a blank document and typing a working title.
- If you want to start exercising, your first step could be putting on your workout shoes.

Make this step so easy that it feels almost laughable. The goal isn't to finish the task today—it's to simply start.

Once you complete that first small step, take a moment to celebrate. Yes, even if it seems tiny. Pat yourself on the back, smile, or say out loud, "I'm making progress."

This simple act of acknowledgment reinforces the idea that you are someone who takes action. And that, my friend, is how momentum begins.

Results of Small Wins

When you consistently build momentum with small actions, something magical happens. Tasks that once felt overwhelming become manageable. Procrastination loses its grip on you, replaced by a growing sense of capability and confidence.

You'll notice that your productivity improves, not because you're working harder, but because you've found a rhythm that works for you. You'll also feel less stress and anxiety because you're no longer haunted by the weight of unfinished tasks.

Most importantly, you'll start to see progress toward your bigger goals. Small steps may feel insignificant at first, but over time, they compound into real, measurable achievements. And as you move forward, you'll realize that overcoming procrastination isn't about transforming your life overnight. It's about making one small, intentional step—every single day.

Closing Thoughts on Chapter 6

Momentum is your greatest ally in the fight against procrastination. By starting small, focusing on quick wins, and letting the snowball effect carry you forward, you'll find yourself achieving more than you ever thought possible.

So today, I challenge you: take one small step toward a goal that matters to you. Start small, build momentum, and watch as those tiny wins pave the way to big success.

Chapter 7: Accountability and Support Systems

Why Accountability Works

"Accountability is one of the most effective tools for overcoming procrastination. But why does it work? The answer lies in psychology. When we share our goals with someone else, we create a sense of external motivation. Suddenly, it's not just about letting ourselves down; there's someone else invested in our success.

This external motivation taps into a powerful part of human nature: our desire for social connection and validation. We are far more likely to follow through on commitments if we know someone will check in on our progress. Accountability isn't about fear or shame—it's about creating a support system that empowers us to show up, even when we don't feel like it."

Building Your Support Network

"Creating a strong support network is a game-changer when tackling procrastination. But where do you start? Begin by identifying people in your life who genuinely want to see you succeed. These could be friends, family members, colleagues, or even mentors. Look for individuals who are reliable, non-judgmental, and willing to hold you accountable without being overly critical.

Once you've identified potential allies, have an honest conversation about your goals. Let them know why their support matters to you and how they can help. For example, you might ask a friend to check in weekly about your progress on a specific project. Or, you could partner with a colleague to exchange updates on shared deadlines.

Remember, accountability is a two-way street. Offer to support your partner in their own goals. This mutual exchange builds trust and strengthens the commitment for both parties."

The Role of Technology

"Technology can be your accountability partner too! In today's digital age, there are countless tools and apps designed to keep you on track. Productivity apps like Trello, Asana, or Todoist allow you to organize tasks and set deadlines. You can even share your progress with others, adding an extra layer of accountability.

For a more personal touch, consider apps like Focusmate, which pairs you with a virtual coworker to work alongside in real-time. Or, use habit-tracking apps like Habitica, which gamify your progress and make it fun to stick to your commitments.

The key is to find tools that align with your personality and preferences. Experiment with a few options, and stick with the ones that genuinely help you stay focused and engaged."

Practical Exercise: Find an Accountability Partner

"Now, let's put this into action with a practical exercise. Follow this step-by-step roadmap to find an accountability partner:

1. **Identify Your Goal** – Write down a specific goal you want to accomplish. Be clear about what success looks like and when you want to achieve it.
2. **List Potential Partners** – Think about people in your life who would make great accountability partners. Choose someone reliable, supportive, and approachable.
3. **Make the Ask** – Reach out to your potential partner and explain what you're working on. Be transparent about how their support could help. For example, you might say, 'I'm working on finishing my project by the end of the month.

Would you be willing to check in with me weekly to make sure I stay on track?'
4. **Set Clear Expectations** – Agree on how and when you'll communicate. Will you check in via text, email, or in-person meetings? Decide on a frequency that feels manageable for both of you.
5. **Commit to Mutual Support** – If they have goals of their own, offer to be their accountability partner too. Supporting each other creates a win-win situation.

Once you've established this relationship, stick to your check-ins. Celebrate your successes together and troubleshoot challenges as a team. With the right accountability partner, you'll find yourself making consistent progress toward your goals."

Results You Can Expect

"When you embrace accountability, you'll notice a shift in how you approach your goals. Tasks that once felt overwhelming become manageable because you're no longer tackling them alone. You'll feel motivated to stay on track, knowing someone else is cheering you on. And as you build momentum, you'll develop the confidence to take on bigger challenges.

But the benefits don't stop there. Accountability strengthens your relationships, too. By inviting others into your journey, you create meaningful connections based on trust and mutual support. It's a simple yet powerful way to overcome procrastination and build a brighter, more productive future."

Chapter 8: Maintaining Long-Term Habits

The key to overcoming procrastination isn't just in taking action today—it's about sustaining those actions tomorrow, next week, and for years to come. In this chapter, we'll explore the science of habit formation, how to prevent relapses, and the importance of reviewing and adjusting your goals. You'll also create a powerful habit tracker to stay consistent and celebrate your progress.

The Science of Habit Formation

Understanding how habits are built and sustained Habits form through a simple but powerful process: **cue, routine, and reward.** Each habit begins with a cue, or trigger, that signals your brain to start the behavior. This leads to the routine—the action itself. Finally, the reward reinforces the behavior, making it more likely to repeat in the future.

For example, let's say you procrastinate on a project. The cue might be the anxiety of starting. The routine becomes avoidance, and the reward is the temporary relief from stress. To build better habits, we need to identify these patterns and replace them with new, productive routines.

How long does it take to form a habit? Contrary to popular belief, habits don't solidify in a fixed number of days. Research shows it can take anywhere from **18 to 254 days** to form a habit, depending on the complexity of the behavior and the individual's circumstances. Consistency is the key.

Preventing Relapses

Strategies for handling setbacks and staying consistent Even with the best intentions, relapses happen. The important thing is to have a plan for getting back on track.

1. **Recognize that setbacks are normal**
   Everyone stumbles. Instead of beating yourself up, view a relapse as a learning opportunity. Ask yourself: What caused the slip, and how can I adjust to prevent it in the future?
2. **Focus on the progress, not perfection**
   Think of habit-building as a marathon, not a sprint. Missing one day doesn't mean you've failed—it just means you're human. The key is to pick up where you left off.
3. **Revisit your "why"**
   Reconnect with your motivation for building the habit. Why does this matter to you? A strong "why" can reignite your drive when you feel stuck.
4. **Have a recovery plan**
   If you miss a day or fall into old habits, decide in advance what you'll do. For example, if you skip your morning writing session, commit to spending 15 minutes writing during lunch or in the evening.

Reviewing and Adjusting Goals

Periodic evaluations to keep your progress aligned Habits evolve over time, and so do your goals. Regularly reviewing your habits ensures they stay aligned with your long-term objectives.

- **Check in weekly**
  Dedicate time each week to reflect on your progress. Ask yourself:
    - Did I stick to my habit this week?
    - What worked well, and what didn't?
    - What changes can I make for next week?
- **Adapt to life changes**
  As circumstances shift, some habits may no longer serve you. For instance, if you change jobs, your time management needs might differ. Be willing to adjust.
- **Celebrate milestones**
  Acknowledge your achievements, no matter how small. This not only boosts morale but reinforces the positive behaviors.

Practical Exercise: Create a Habit Tracker

A system to track and maintain your productivity habits
Tracking your habits makes your progress visible and motivates you to stay consistent. Here's how to create an effective habit tracker:

16. **Choose your format**

    - Use a notebook, planner, or digital app to track your habits.
    - Create a simple table with the habit name on one side and days of the week across the top.

17. **List your key habits**
Write down 3–5 habits you want to track. For example:

    - Spend 20 minutes planning your day each morning.
    - Complete one small task before lunch.
    - Review your weekly goals every Sunday.

18. **Mark your progress daily**
Each day, check off the habits you complete. Seeing those marks accumulate provides a sense of accomplishment.

19. **Reflect monthly**
At the end of each month, review your tracker. Which habits are solidifying? Which need more focus? Adjust your strategy accordingly.

Results: A Life Transformed by Consistent Habits

When you follow these strategies, you'll develop habits that transform your relationship with time, productivity, and procrastination. Over time, these changes won't feel like forced routines—they'll become second nature. You'll experience:

7. **Increased confidence** in tackling tasks head-on.
8. **Reduced stress** as you spend less energy worrying and more energy doing.

9. **Stronger discipline** that carries over into all areas of your life.

Remember, the goal isn't perfection—it's progress. Celebrate your journey and keep building habits that align with the life you want to create.

www.ingramcontent.com/pod-product-compliance
Lightning Source LLC
Chambersburg PA
CBHW030106230526
45471CB00003B/1285